A Complete Guide to Stenography

A

COMPLETE GUIDE

TO

STENOGRAPHY,

OR AN

ENTIRE NEW SYSTEM

OF

WRITING SHORT HAND.

FOR THE USE OF SCHOOLS AND PRIVATE TUITION.

BY T. TOWNDROW,

PROFESSOR AND TEACHER OF STENOGRAPHY.

" Despair of nothing you would attain,
Unwearied diligence your point will gain."

SECOND EDITION.

NEW HAVEN:

HEZEKIAH HOWE.

NEW YORK—JOCELYN, DARLING & CO.

1832.

Entered according to the Act of Congress, in the year 1832, by
THOMAS TOWNDROW, in the Clerk's office, of the District Court of
Connecticut.

Printed by Hezekiah Howe.

PREFACE.

THE Author takes great pleasure in laying before the public, a second edition of his Complete Guide to Stenography, or an entire new system of writing Short-Hand; founded on principles more simple and comprehensive, than any that has heretofore made its appearance. The author can, with confidence, assure the purchaser of this *second edition* of his work, that the whole has been carefully revised, and such additional illustrations and plates of examples have been introduced, as his diligence has enabled him to procure.

The system which most simplifies the art, and renders it more easily acquired and practised, must be regarded as preferable; and this edition, small as it may appear, will be found to possess those advantages, and it is believed, to contain all that is requisite to produce an accomplished short hand writer. Indeed, the author has made it his incessant study to render the system not only the most easy to be comprehended and learned, but to bring its acquisition within the pecuniary means of every inquiring and intelligent young person.

To those masters who have introduced this treatise into their schools, the author considers himself under particular obligations, and he doubts not that an art of such confessed utility, and easy acquirement, will, in a short time, become as generally practised by those preparing for College or other professional studies, as common writing. Those instructors who have not yet become acquainted with the utility of this manual as a class book, are respectfully invited to examine it, and inform themselves of the many and great advantages arising from the practice of Stenography, which are thus eloquently and forcibly stated by Mr. Gawtress, in his excellent introduction to Byrom.

" A practical acquaintance with this art is highly favorable to the improvement of the mind, invigorating all its faculties, and drawing forth all its resources. The close attention that is requisite in following the

voice of a speaker induces habits of patience, perseverance, and watch-
fulness, which will gradually extend themselves to other pursuits and
avocations, and at length inure the writer to exercise them on every
occasion in life. When writing in public, it will also be absolutely necessary to distinguish and adhere to the train of thought which runs
through the discourse, and to observe the modes of its connexion. This
will naturally have a tendency to endue the mind with quickness of
apprehension, and will impart an habitual readiness and distinctness of
perception, as well as a methodical simplicity of arrangement, which
cannot fail to conduce greatly to mental superiority. The judgment
will be strengthened and the taste refined; and the practitioner will by
degrees become habituated to seize the original and leading parts of a
discourse or harangue, and to reject whatever is common-place, trivial,
or uninteresting.

"The advantages of short-hand, in cases where *secrecy* is required,
are sufficiently obvious. It is true, that when a system is made public,
this effect is partially destroyed. Yet it seldom happens that steno-
graphic memorandums fall into the hands of those who can read them ;
and when the writer has any reason to anticipate such an occurrence, it
will be easy, after learning a good system, so to transpose a few of the
Arbitraries, as to render the writing illegible to all but himself.

"The *facility it affords to the acquisition of learning*, ought to render it an indispensable branch in the education of youth. To be enabled
to treasure up for future study, the substance of lectures, sermons, &c.,
is an accomplishment attended with such evident advantages, that it
stands in no need of recommendation. Nor is it a matter of small im-
portance, that by this Art the youthful student is furnished with an easy
means of making a number of valuable extracts in the moments of leis-
ure, and thus lay up a stock of knowledge for his future occasions.

"The *memory* is also improved by the practice of Stenography. The
obligation the writer is under to retain in his mind the last sentence of
the speaker, at the same time he is attending to the following one, must
be highly beneficial to that faculty, which more than any owes its improvement to exercise. And so much are the powers of retention

strengthened and expanded by this exertion, that a practical Stenographer will frequently recollect more without writing, than a person unacquainted with the Art could copy in the time by the use of common hand."

"The rapidity with which it enables a person to commit his own thoughts to the safety of manuscript, also renders it an object peculiarly worthy of regard. By this means a thousand ideas which daily strike us, and which are lost before we can record them in the usual way, may be snatched from destruction, and preserved till mature deliberation can ripen and perfect them."

The following extract is from the pen of T. CAMPBELL, Esq., Lord Rector of Glasgow University.

"I should exhort all young men to learn *that most useful Art*, SHORTHAND WRITING; an Art which, I believe, will one day be studied as universally as common writing, and which will abridge the labor of penmanship, to a degree that will materially quicken the intercourse of human thought."

NEW HAVEN, 1832.

1*

ADVERTISEMENT.

IT being the intention of the Author, to visit the CITIES and PRINCIPAL TOWNS in the UNITED STATES, previous to his return to EUROPE, he would most respectfully inform those persons, who may feel desirous of receiving instructions from him, wherever he may be; that he will give them a complete knowledge of this pleasing and very useful art, in a brief but interesting course of *six easy lessons*, in accordance with the exercises of this work; and should the purchaser of this book, desire additional examples, or explanations on the subject, he will readily afford what assistance his engagements will permit.

STENOGRAPHY.

ALPHABETICAL CHARACTERS, and the words they represent, when written singly or stand alone.

A or E	.	Ah, at, am, and,
B	⌐	Be, by, been, but,
D	/	Do, does, did, done,
F or V	\	For, from, of, if,
or S	⌐	God, give, go, gone,
H	⌐	Have, he, had, how,
K or	⌐	Keep, could, can, knew,
L	(	Lord, all, let, like,
M	◡	Him, me, my, may,
N	∪	An, in, not, no,
O or U	,	Oh, on, out, ought,
P	¦	Put, power, up, upon,
Q	⌒	Quick, question, quite, quantity,
R	/	Are, art, or, our,
S, C or	∩	So, is, as, us,
T	—	To, it, that, the,
W	◡	We, was, with, will,
X	∪	Except, expect, exceed, example,
Y or I	⌐	Ye, yet, you, your,
Wh	⌐	Who, why, when, what,
Ch	⌐	Which, much, each, such,
Sh	/	She, shall, shame, should,
Th	/	Thee, they, thou, them,
Thr	·—	There, either, their, therefore,

REMARKS TO THE LEARNER.

THE pupil must commit to memory the Alphabetical characters, and the words they represent when standing alone, so as to be enabled to note down with facility, the character which stands in the same line as the word intended to be written.

The small dot placed near each character, is to show at which point the pupil must commence to form them.

Be as exact as possible in the form and position of every character.

The pupil should accustom himself to write the short hand small and neat; and not be too anxious about writing expeditiously at first.

OF JOINING CONSONANTS.

When *b*, precedes any of the following letters, *k, m, q, r, sk, sm, sq,* or *sr,* it must be made thus : ⟍ commencing at the top, as in *book, basket, observe,* &c. In all other cases that in the alphabet must be made use of. To express *bb*, it must be written thus : ⟋⟍ *bb*, as in *Babylon,* &c.

When it is necessary to write *dd,* the usual character for *d,* must be written twice. Ex. ⅔ *ndd,* for *ended.*

To express *ff,* or *fv,* the character for *f,* must be made twice its usual length as in *fifth, favor,* &c.

When it is necessary to write *gg, mm, nn, pp, xx,* or *yi,* the character for *g, m, n, p, x,* or *y,* must be written twice without lifting the pen, thus : ⌣‗ *gg,* &c. (See page 8. Rule 4.)

The character for *k,* may be made down when preceding any of the following letters, *m, q, r, t,* and *y.* In all other cases it must be made up. *kk,* may be written thus : ⅇ

R, when combined with any other consonant, must be made thus: / the same form as *d*, commencing at the bottom. Ex. ᕓ *frst*, first; ᕓᕁ *frnd*, friend, &c. To express *rr*, the pupil must make the short hand *r*, and a small common *r*, at the top. Ex. ᕞ *err*, error; ᕝ *brr*, bearer, &c.

To express *ss*, the small circle for *s* must be made twice its usual size.

To express *tt*, one must be written under the other, as in the following examples: ᗒ *ttl*, title; ᗑ *stt*, state, &c.

The double consonant *sh*, may be made either upwards or downwards, that which is most convenient to join to the preceding or following character. Ex. �╱ *dsh*, dash; ᕥ *prsh*, perish, &c.

RULES FOR WRITING.

I. Spell as you pronounce, then every silent letter will be omitted, and one letter will be frequently substituted for another. Write no more letters than is just necessary to give the sound of the word.

II. Let each word be completely finished before the pen is taken off the paper.

III. *C* and *z* are rejected in Short-hand; *c* having both a hard and soft sound similar to *k* and *s*; as in compel, *kmpl*; facility, *fslity*; certain, *srtn*, &c.—they will supply its place according to its sound—and *z* being similar in sound to *s*, the latter is always substituted.

IV. When two consonants of the same kind or sound come together, without any vowel between them, only *one* is to be expressed. *Ex.* ᕚ *btr*, better; ᕦ *sfr*, suffer, &c. But if a vowel or vowels intervene, both are written. *Ex.* ᕗ *sstr*, sister; ᕘ *lnn*, linen; ᕙ *mmry*, memory, &c.

V. The letters *cks*, and *cts*, may be called *x*. *Ex.* ᕜ *rx*, rocks; ᕝ *ax*, acts, &c. *ks*, may be also called *x*, as in for*ks*, wor*ks*, &c.

VI. When the consonants *gh* meet together they are not to be written unless sounding like *f*, which letter is then written in their place. *Ex.* ∧ *rf*, rou*gh*; ⌣ *enf*, enou*gh*, &c.

VII. The double consonant *gh* may always be omitted when *i* precedes or *t* follows. *Ex.* ⤳ *lit*, light; ⤳ *nit*, night, &c.

VIII. *Ph* sounds like *f*, and may be represented by that letter. *Ex.* Philosopher, *flsfr*; *ph*antom, *fntm*, &c.

IX. The diphthongs *ue*, *ui*, *ou*, and *ough*, generally sound like *w*; and in that case *w* may be substituted. *Ex.* ⤳ *frwt*, fru*i*t; ⤳ *trw*, true; ⤳ *thw*, thou*gh*, &c.

X. The vowels *a*, *e*, *o*, and *u*, are never used in spelling, except when distinctly sounded at the beginning or end of words. *Ex.* ⤳ *atnd*, attend; ⤳ *obsrv*, observe; ⤳ *tre*, tree; ⤳ *othr*, other, &c.

XI. The character for *ch*, is not used in spelling, only when it has its natural sound, as in charm, chapter, change, chosen, &c. When *ch* sounds like *k*, the latter is always substituted, as in *ch*ymist *kmst*; Christ, *krst*, &c.

XII. *B*, *d*, *g*, *k*, and *w*, may be omitted in such words as the following: remember, *rmmr*; friendship, *frnship*; strength, *strnth*; thankful, *thn-ful*; answer, *nsr*, &c.

XIII. The letters *cu* sound like *q*, and may be represented by that letter, as in cure, *qr*; obscure, *obsqr*; elocution, *lq-tion*, &c.

XIV. *D*, at the end of words, if it be more plain and easy, may be written *t*. *Ex.* Expressed, *xprst*; distressed, *dstrst*, &c.

EXERCISE I.

The pupil is requested to write the following words in Short-hand as abbreviated in *Italics*.

Must	*mst*	possess	*pss*
first	*frst*	inspire	*nspr*
friend	*frnd*	minister	*mnstr*
stand	*stnd*	gospel	*gspl*
master	*mstr*	appear	*apr*
deliver	*dlvr*	among	*amng*
grant	*grnt*	philosopher	*flsfr*
utmost	*utmst*	phlegm	*flm*
parent	*prnt*	strength	*strnth*
mind	*mnd*	mercy	*mrsy*
tender	*tndr*	honor	*onr*
render	*rndr*	excuse	*xqs*
before	*bfr*	cistern	*sstrn*
govern	*grvrn*	impeach	*mpch*
forth	*frth*	liberal	*lbrl*
express	*xprs*	vessel	*vsl*
despair	*dspr*	after	*ftr*
trust	*trst*	farewell	*frwl*
watch	*wch*	instant	*nstnt*
general	*gnrl*	paper	*ppr*
envy	*nv*	endeavor	*ndvr*
energy	*nrg*	people	*ppl*
excess	*xs*	purpose	*prps*
excel	*xl*	pillow	*plo*
empty	*mt*	domestic	*dmstk*
animal	*nml*	success	*skss*
person	*prsn*	mistake	*mstk*
system	*sstm*	distant	*dstnt*
kind	*knd*	sight	*sit*
exist	*xst*	benefit	*bnft*
extent	*xtnt*	against	*agnst*
teach	*tch*	cure	*qr*
custom	*kstm*	change	*chng*

Pl.3

PREPOSITIONS. .

⌐	Con, Contra, contri, contro,
⌐	Com, compre, compla, compli,
⌐	Disen, disin, discom, discon,
\	Affec, afflic, effec,
—	Aggra, aggree, agree, agri,
(	Magni, multi, misin, miscon,
)	Enter, inter, intro, intru,
┆	Pre, pri, pro, per,
⌐	Recom, recon, repre, repro,
°	Circum, signis, sub, sup, super,
—	Tran, trans, temp, tempt,
⌣	Exer, exter, extra, extre,

TERMINATIONS. .

⌐	Ble, bled, able, ably, ible, ibly,
\	Form, ful, fully, ference,
?	Ify, ity, iety, ing, ingly,
(	Lity, tial, ally, ly, less,
(	Mand, mend, ment,-ed,
⌣	Ance, ence, iance, ience,-cy, ant, ent-ly,
°	Tion, ution, ition, otion, ution,
°	Ship, self, selves,
—	Tive, active, ective, ictive, uctive,
\	Ward, wards, warded, wardeth,
⌣	Act, ect, ict, uct, ed, ly,
—	Ate, ated, ately, sionate, sionately,
—	Eous, ious, uous, cously, cousness.

.See notes p. n.

Notes to Plate III.

I. When a word commences with a *prefix* or *preposition*,[*] and ends without a termination, the pupil must first write the preposition, and finish the word by writing the consonants following, which are fully sounded. *Ex.* ⌐√ *trns*-fr, transfer; ᵔ— *inter*-st, interest; /⸗/ *compre*-nd, comprehend, &c.

II. When a word ends with a termination without commencing with a preposition; first write the consonants which are fully sounded, and finish the word by making the termination mark. *Ex.* /᷅ D-*mand*, demand; ⸗ V-*sion*, vision; ∨⅄ Fr-*ful*, fearful, &c.

III. When a word commences with a preposition, and ends with a termination, both must be written, and denoted by placing a period over the word, which saves half the time that would be required in making both preposition and termination marks. *Ex.* ⌐ⸯ *Inter-ment*, interment; ⸗/⹁ *Temp-r-ance*, temperance; ⸺ᵒ *Tempt-ation*, temptation, &c.

IV. But when a word has two of such terminations as have been selected, the first must then be spelt according to its sound, and the last denoted by its usual mark. *Ex.* ⌐⸝⹁ *Trans*-fm-*ation*, transformation; /ⸯ *Com*-nd-*ment*, commandment; /⹁ *recom*-nd-*ation*, recommendation, &c.

V. The termination *eth*, may be denoted by a small scratch made through the last consonant, when more easy made than the character for *th*. *Ex.* ⸗ᵣ St-*eth*, sitteth; ⸗⸝⸢ Trst-*eth*, trusteth, &c.

VI. The termination mark for *tion, ation*, &c. is not confined to those terminations alone, but may be used for other terminations of the same sound: as *sion, cian*, &c.

VII. When *c* precedes *tion*, it may be written *x*, as *xion*; the *ion* being expressed by the charactor for *tion*; as in detruction, dstr*xion*; reflection, rfl*xion*, &c.

---

[*] The prepositions and terminations referred to in this treatise are only such as have been selected on Plate III.

ABBREVIATIONS, &C.

(1) / Placed near a character, represents an antithesis, or opposition of words. *Ex.* ⅄ Good *and-bad,* ⎷ Life *and-death,* ⅄ Summer *and-winter,* &c.

(2) ── Placed under a word, denotes a repetition of words or sentence. *Ex.* ⊸ The Lord *of-lords,* ⌒ From time *to-time,* &c.

(3) ⸍ Placed over a word, shews it to be the name of a person or place. *Ex.* ⸜ ⸝ Thomas Jefferson, ⸝ Boston, ⸝ Salem, &c.

(4) ⸍ Placed under a word, shews it to be a very unusual word, or a word very much abbreviated. *Ex.* ⌐ peculiar, ⸜ misrepresentation, &c.

(5) ⸌ Signifies a defect in the writing—either that something is there omitted, or doubtfully expressed.

(6) ∘ Placed over or under a word, denote the prepositions *over, under, above* and *below. Ex.* ⸝ *over*-turn, ⸝ *under*-take, ⸝ *above-the.*

(7) ⸌ *Au, aw,* or *augh,* as in a*u*thor, a*w*ful, ta*ugh*t, &c.

(8) ⸌ Semicolon, or colon.

(9) × A period, or full stop.

(10) ? ! A note of interrogation or admiration may be denoted by its usual mark.

(11) ⸝ *I, eye, high,* ⸝ &c. ⊂ *viz.*

(12) ♂ Mark of reference, for marginal notes or observations.

(13) ℘ Repetition of text, &c.

EXERCISE II.

To be written in Short-hand. (Psalm cxxxvi.)

1. O give thanks unto the Lord; for he is good: for his
   O give thnks nto *the Lord; for he is* gd: *for* hs
mercy endureth for ever.
mrsy ndr*eth for* evr.

2. O give thanks unto the God of gods: for his mercy
   O give thnks nto *the God of-gods: for* hs mrsy
endureth for ever.
ndr*eth for* evr.

3. O give thanks unto the Lord of lords: for his mercy
   O give thnks nto *the Lord of-lords:* for hs mrsy
endureth for ever.
ndr*eth for* evr.

4. To him who doeth great wonders: for his mercy en-
   To him who dth grt wndrs: *for* hs mrsy n-
dureth for ever.
dr*eth for* evr.

5. To him that by wisdom made the heavens: for his
   To him that by wsdm md *the* hvns: *for* hs
mercy endureth for ever.
mrsy ndr*eth for* evr.

6. To him that stretched out the earth above the waters:
   To him that strchd *out the* rth *above-the* wtrs:
for his mercy endureth for ever.
for hs mrsy ndr*eth for* evr.

7. To him that made great lights: for his mercy endureth
   To him that md grt lits: *for* hs mrsy ndr*eth*
or ever.
or evr.

8. The sun to rule by day: for his mercy endureth for ever.
   The sn *to* rl *by* dy: *for* hs mrsy ndr*eth for* evr.

EXERCISE III.

The following words to be written in Short Hand.

Prepositions in Italics.

Contend	*Con*-tnd	Interview	*Inter*-vw
Confer	*Con*-fr	Prefer	*Pre*-fr
Contrary	*Contra*-ry	Profess	*Pro*-fs
Contriver	*Contri*-vr	Preserve	*Pre*-srv
Controversy	*Contro*-vrsy	Recompense	*Recom*-pns
Compare	*Com*-pr	Reconcile	*Recon*-sl
Comprehensive	*Compre*-nsv	Reprehend	*Repre*-nd
Disinter	*Disin*-tr	Superfine	*Super*-fn
Discontent	*Discon*-tnt	Transfer	*Trans*-fr
Affected	*Affec*-td	Tranquil	*Tran*-ql
Aggravate	*Aggra*-vt	Tempest	*Temp*-st
Misinfer	*Misin*-fr	Temper	*Temp*-r
Multitude	*Multi*-td	External	*Exter*-nl
Interest	*Inter*-st	Undertake	*Under*-tk
Interfere	*Inter*-fr	Understand	*Under*-stnd
Entertain	*Enter*-tn	Overwhelm	*Over*-wlm

Terminations in Italics.

Miserable	msr-*able*	Differently	dfr-*ently*
Humble	m-*ble*	Nation	n-*ation*
Gamble	gm-*ble*	Petition	pt-*tion*
Inform	n-*form*	Dimension	dmn-*sion*
Reform	r-*form*	Relation	rl-*ation*
Powerful	pr-*ful*	Friendship	frn-*ship*
Merciful	mrs-*ful*	Themselves	thm-*selves*
Missing	ms-*ing*	Attractive	atr-*active*
Expressing	xprs-*ing*	Destructive	dstr-*uctive*
Felicity	fls-*ity*	Toward	t-*ward*
Demand	d-*mand*	Exact	x-*act*
Testament	tst-*ment*	Detect	dt-*ect*
Sentiment	snt-*ment*	Pious	p-*ious*
Eminence	mn-*ence*	Gracious	gra-*ious*
Judgment	jg-*ment*	Righteousness	rit-*eousnes*
Endurance	ndr-*ance*	Trusteth	trst-*eth*
Sufficiency	sfs-*iency*	Giveth	gv-*eth*

Prepositions and Terminations in Italics.

Interference	*inter-ference*
Transform	*trans-form*
Tempting	*tempt-ing*
Temptation	*tempt-ation*
Interment	*inter-ment*
Interring	*inter-ing*
Misinform	*misin-form*
Perform	*per-form*
Discommend	*discom-mend*
Commence	*com-ence*
Recommend	*recom-mend*
Command	*com-mand*
Exertion	*exer-tion*
Circumference	*circum-ference*
Affection	*affec-tion*
Affectionate	*affec-tionate*
Presumption	*presmtion*
Temperance	*temprance*
Transportation	*transprtation*
Translation	*translation*
Transferring	*transfring*
Interesting	*intersting*
Comprehension	*comprension*
Multipresence	*multiprsence*
Persecution	*persqtion*
Promotion	*promotion*
Compassion	*compsion*
Signification	*signifktion*
Transposing	*transpsing*
Tempestuous	*tempstuous*
Circumstance	*circumtance*
Aggregation	*aggregation*
Contemptuous	*contmtuous*

ARBITRARIES.

The following are a few *Arbitraries*, or *natural contractions*, which may be used at the option of the pupil.

a__	Long, along,	/.	Broken, separated,
@	About, around,	≠	Undivide-d, unbroken,
⋒	Round, roundabout,	$	Thank–s–ed–giving,
+	Cross, across, crossways,	⤬	Encroachment,
≠	The cross of Christ,	ഄ	Nevertheless,
⌣	Christian, christianity,	⫨	Character–ize–istic,
⊬	Anti-christ,	⋏	Notwithstanding,
⊬	Glory—ify—ious	ɣ	Distinguish–ed–ing
⊬	Heaven-ly,	⌒	Discover–disclose–d–ing,
⌣	Jehovah,	⋔	Remark–ed–ing–able,
D	Jesus Christ,	⊣	Contrary, contradict-ion,
:	Holy Ghost, Holy Spirit,	⌣	Extraordinary,
"	Grace of God,	Ψ	Unnatural, uncommon,
⋹	Crucify, crucifixion,	{	Tremble- shake,-d–ing,
ƒ	Creator, creation,	aa	Company, accompany-ied,
⊦	Spiritual, sacramental,	O	Nothing, nobody,
⋗	Everlasting, eternity,	⊙	Something, somebody,
Z	Zeal-ous-ously-ousness,	⊖	Through,
⌞	Within,	⊖	Throughout,
⌝	Without,	⊕	The world,
⌐	Behind,	—⧈	Right hand,
⋏	Betwixt, between,	⧈—	Left hand,
⌐	Beneath, underneath,	⋌	Legislature,
=	Together,	H	House of representatives,
⌣	Altogether,	△	Commonwealth.

N. B. The names of the several States of the Union, may be written in Long-hand, with their usual abbreviations; as, *Ms.* for Massachusetts, *N. Y.* for New York, *Va.* for Virginia, *N. E.* for New England, *U. S.* for United States, &c.

EXAMPLES.

I

By the fear of the Lord men depart
from evil. It is good for me to draw
near to God. Be ye also ready. They
that sow in tears shall reap in joy.
All things work together for good
to them that love God. If God be
for us who can be against us.

II

Make a joyful noise unto the Lord
all ye lands. Serve the Lord with
gladness come before his presence
with singing Know ye that the Lord
he is God it is he that hath made us
and not we ourselves we are his
people and the sheep of his pasture.

III

Turn ye, turn ye from your evil
ways for why will ye die O house
of Israel? Sorrow is better than
laughter for by the sadness of
the countenance the heart is made
better. Precious in the sight of
the Lord is the death of his
saints. Praise ye the Lord.

IV

SHORTENING RULES,

For enabling the Writer to follow the most rapid Speaker.

I. The first word or two of every sentence should be written very plain, so as to leave them distinct and of an easy legibility. By this means you will secure connexion, and render the whole sentence easy to be read, though much abbreviated in the latter part.

II. The articles *a, an* and *the,* and the sign of the genitive case, *of,* may be always omitted.

III. The sign of the plural of nouns, together with *s, eth, ed,* and *est* terminations in the tenses of verbs may be omitted.

IV. Some words of more than one termination, may have their termination expressed by the defective sign. But the termination must never be omitted if a long vowel goes before.

V. In many cases the terminations are so that no expression need be made for them.

VI. Many words may be expressed by their first vowel and consonant following.

VII. The first consonant and termination of a word is often sufficient to express the whole.

VIII. The radical part of a word may often express the whole word: as *pq* for *peculiar—xp* for *expense—mp* for *employ.*

IX. Not only are all mutes or unsounding letters to be excluded, but even some sounding consonants may be dropped, and oftentimes one letter that is more proper may be substituted for one that is less so; this rule may be extended or contracted, according to the capacity of the writer.

X. All proper names of persons or places, and likewise technical terms often occurring, may be expressed, (after the first or second time of using,) by their initial and termin-

2*

ating character, or with the defective sign placed under their initial.

XI. Long words will frequently admit of large contractions ; generally one or two syllables may be dropped before the termination *tion*, and other terminations in long words.

XII. A number of small words in most sentences may by omitted, without affecting the sense of the passage, or even rendering doubtful the exact expression used.

XIII. Such words as are usually abbreviated in long hand may be abbreviated in short-hand.

XIV. Poetic contractions may also be made use of: as, *morn*, for *morning*, &c.

XV. Some compound words may be written singly, thus: *with-draw*, *child-hood*, *ever-more*, &c.

XVI. When a sentence is repeated, and not repeated till something else occurs, write down a word or two and make the mark for *&c.*

Exercise IV.

Thanksgiving.—Crafts.

It is a wise and venerable custom, in New-England, to
It is a ws *and* vnrable kstm *in* N. E.* *to*
set apart one day in the year for the voluntary commemora-
st aprt wn dy *in the* yr *for the* vlntry com-mra-
tion of the divine favor, and goodness ; and it is pleasing to
tion *of the* dvn fvr *and* gdns ; *and it is* plsing *to*
see so correct a custom gaining ground in our country.
se *so* kreot *a* kstm gning grnd *in our* kntry.

Not that in New England, or any where else, it requires
Not that in N. E. *or* ny whr ls *it* rqrs

---

* See list of Arbitraries, &c. (p. 16.)

a year to roll over our heads to convince us of the everlast-
a yr *to* rl *over-our* hds *to convns us of the everlast-*
ing mercies of Heaven.
ing mrss *of Heaven.*

The sublime structure of the universe; this beautiful
The sublm strktr *of the* univrs; ths btf*ul*
landscape, the earth; the magnificent ocean, now assailing
lndskp *the* rth; *the* mgnfsent oshn nw asli*ng*
the clouds with its foam, and then nestling the little birds
the klds *with* ts fm *and* thn nstli*ng the* ltl brds
on its billows; the glorious sun, and these sweet sentinels
on ts blws; *the glorious* sn *and* ths swt sntnls
of light, the stars; the voice of thunder, and the song of the
of lit *the* strs; *the* vs *of* thndr *and the* sng *of the*
linnet; who knows any thing of these, and can for a
lint; *who* kn*ws* ny thi*ng of* ths *and can for a*
moment doubt the supreme benevolence of the Almighty!
m*ment* dt *the* sprm bnvle*nce of the* Almit!

Yet, although every instant be fruitful in blessings, we
Yet lthw *every* nstnt *be* frwtf*ul in* blsi*ngs we*
are inattentive, and do not regard; we are ignorant, and do
are ntntv *and do not* rgrd; *we are* ignra*nt and do*
not appreciate; we are ungrateful, and do not consider; we
not aprsiate; *we are* ungrtf*ul and do not* consdr; *we*
are selfish, and will not understand them. The best require
are slfsh *and will not* understnd *them. The* bst rqr
to be reminded of their duty, and the thoughtless must be
to be rmndd *of their* dty *and the* thtls mst *be*
told of it always.
tld *of it* lwys.

It is wise, therefore, to select the season of gladness, and
It is ws *therefore to* slect *the* ssn *of* gldns *and*
point to the source of good.
pnt *to the* srs *of* gd.

When the husbandman rejoices for the harvest is ripe,
When the hsbndmn   rjss *for the*   rvst *is* rp
and the poor go into the field to glean
and the pr *go* nto *the* fld *to* gln

The sheaves, which God ordains to bless
The shvs *which God* ordus *to* bls
The widow, and the fatherless,
The wdo *and the* fthrls,

it becomes man to acknowledge the reward of his labors,
it bkms   mn *to*   aknlg   *the* rward *of* hs lbrs,
the blessings, of his hopes, and the goodness of the giver
the bls*ings* *of* hs hps *and the* gdns   *of the* gvr
of all things. Then, especially, should he pour forth the
of all thi*ngs.* Thn   esps*ally* *should he* pr   frth *the*
grateful incense of his praise, and his devotion.
grt*ful* nsns *of* hs prs   *and* hs dv*tion.*

The Almighty deserves the praise of his creatures. The
The Almit   dsrvs   *the* prs *of* hs *creatures.* *The*
flower pays its worship in fragrant exhalation, and the lark
flwr pys ts wr*ship* *in* frgr*ant*   xl*ation*   *and the* lrk
when he carols at the gate of heaven, in praise of their glo-
when he krls *at the* gt *of heaven* *in* prs *of their glo-*
rious Maker. The sun burns incense daily, and the virgin
rious Mkr.   *The* sn brns nsns   d*ly* *and the* vrgn
stars keep nightly vigils; the mysterious anthem of the
strs *keep* nit*ly*   vgls; *the* mstri*ous*   nthm *of the*
forest proclaim its devotion, and the sea declares its obedi-
frst *proklm* ts dv*otion* *and the* se   dklrs   ts obd-
ence as it murmurs into repose.
ience as it mrmrs   nto rps.

Every moment of time bears an errand of mercy, and
Evry m*ment* *of* tm brs *an* ernd *of* mrsy   *and*
should not be allowed to pass without an acknowledgment
should not be alwd   *to* ps *without an*   aknlg*ment*
of gratitude,
of grttd.

TRANSLATION OF THE FRONTISPIECE.

The Ten Commandments.

1. Thou shalt have none other gods but me.

2. Thou shalt not make to thyself any graven image, nor he likeness of any thing that is in heaven above, or in the arth beneath, or in the water under the earth. Thou shalt lot bow down to them nor worship them: For I the Lord hy God am a jealous God; and visit the sins of the fathers ipon the children, unto the third and fourth generation of hem that hate me; and show mercy unto thousands in them hat love me, and keep my commandments.

3. Thou shalt not take the name of the Lord thy God in 'ain: For the Lord will not hold him guiltless that taketh iis name in vain.

4. Remember that thou keep holy the Sabbath-day. Six lays shalt thou labor, and do all that thou hast to do; but he seventh day is the Sabbath of the Lord thy God. In it hou shalt do no manner of work; thou, and thy son, and hy daughter, thy man-servant, and thy maid-servant, thy attle, and the stranger that is within thy gates. For in six lays the Lord made heaven and earth, the sea, and all that n them is, and rested the seventh day: wherefore the Lord lessed the seventh day, and hallowed it.

5. Honor thy father and thy mother; that thy days may e long in the land which the Lord thy God giveth thee.

6. Thou shalt do no murder.

7. Thou shalt not commit adultery.

8. Thou shalt not steal.

9. Thou shalt not bear false witness against thy neighbor.

10. Thou shalt not covet thy neighbor's house, thou shalt lot covet thy neighbor's wife, nor his servant, nor his maid, ior his ox, nor his ass, nor any thing that is his.

"All things whatsoever ye would that men s
unto you, do ye even so to them : for this is the
the prophets."

"We hold these truths to be self-evident : That
are created equal ; that they are endowed by their
with certain unalienable rights ; that among these
liberty, and the pursuit of happiness."

Translation of Specimen 4. *Plate* 4. (Psalm

1. O come, *let us sing* unto *the Lord : let us* mal
ful noise to the rock *of our salvation.* 2. *Let us*
fore his presence *with thanksgiving, and* make
noise unto *him with* psalms. 3. *For the Lord is*
God, *and a* great King *above all* gods. 4. *In* his
the deep places *of the* earth : *the* strength *of the* hi
also. 5. *The* sea *is* his, *and he* made *it : and* h
formed *the* dry land. 6. *O* come, *let us* worship
down : *let us* kneel before *the Lord our* maker. 7
is our God ; and we are the people of his pasture,
sheep *of* his hand. To-day, *if ye will* hear his v
Harden *not your* heart, *as in the* day *of provocation*
in the day *of temptation in the* wilderness : 9
your fathers *tempted me,* proved *me, and* saw *my* we
Forty years long *was I* grieved *with* this general
said, *It is a* people *that do* err *in their* heart, *and* t
not known *my* ways : 11. Unto whom *I* sware *in* a
that they should not enter into *my* rest.

MISCELLANEOUS RULES AND DIRECTIONS.

In the study of this work, the pupil is recommended after having committed to memory the alphabetical characters, their names and the words they represent when written singly or standing alone, to exercise himself in combining the various letters of the alphabet backwards and forwards, till he has become fully acquainted with the method of joining the consonants, and forming the words with ease and expedition; when this is acquired, he may begin to take notes from any deliberate speaker, or procure a friend to read for him, each time transcribing his notes into long hand, before he attempts to write again; by this means the characters will become perfectly familiar to the pupil, and in a little time he will be enabled to read his Short Hand manuscript, without the least difficulty.

In reading Short Hand, every consonant should be sounded fully and strongly: This will suggest to the reader the vowels omitted, and greatly assist in decyphering.

When a word is not known at first sight, proceed to speak each letter separately and distinctly, and then pronounce the whole together—thus: *n, v*, when pronounced *nv* would give the word *envy*—*n, r, g*, pronounced *nrg* would be *energy*—*dk*, for *decay*, &c.*

When the learner first attends a Court of Justice, or other public place, in order to take notes, he should not attempt to write the whole, but merely the heads of what is then said. It is natural to suppose, that he will at first be somewhat confused, which may prevent him from writing with that degree of ease or expedition which he has been able to do when alone; but he ought to guard against this timidity,

---

* *Mt*, may also be applied in the same manner as follows:—
   The coach is quite *mt*, (empty.)

and not suffer himself in the least to be discouraged, though
he should fail in his first or second attempt; but let him per-
severe, and a little practice of this kind, will soon enable
him to write the whole of what is delivered.

When the writer goes over the discourse again, it will be
well for him to put in the articles or other small words he
may have omitted, and if he perceives any little obscurity;
so as to make it quite complete, and easy to be read at any
future time.

It will facilitate the progress of the learner, if, when he
casts his eye on an unusual word, or hears it spoken in com-
pany, he accustom himself to consider how it should be expressed in short hand. This method will greatly contribute
to readiness and expedition.

OF TEACHING.

The assistance of a teacher, when it can be obtained, is of
great advantage in the study of this art. Men differ in their
genius and perceptions, and every pupil has his own peculiar views and ideas. Difficulties present themselves to some
minds which never occur to others, and which no writer on
the subject can anticipate. It is impossible, in a public treatise, to lay down the rules and explanations adapted to the
capacities, and satisfactory to the understanding of all who
may endeavor to learn by it. A master, however, has it in
his power to give such minute and personal instructions as
cannot fail to produce a beneficial result. He can at once
explain to the student whatever seems obscure and ambigu-
ous; he can solve his difficulties, correct his mistakes, assist his inventions, encourage him in his progress, and lead
him on to a practical proficiency.

EXERCISE V.

Conclusion of a Discourse delivered at Plymouth, Mass. Dec. 22d. 1820, in commemoration of the first settlement in New-England.—By DANIEL WEBSTER.

Let us not forget *the* reli*gious character of our* origin. *Our* fathers were brought hither *by* their *high* vener*ation* *for the Christian* religion. *They* journeyed *in* its light, *and* *labored in* its hope. *They* sought *to* incorporate its prin*ciples with the* elements *of their* society, *and to* diffuse its *influence* through *all their* insti*tutions*, civil, political *and* *literary.* *Let us* cherish these senti*ments, and* extend *their* *influence* still more widely; in the full conviction that that *is* *the* happiest soc*iety which* partakes *in the* highest degree *of the* mild *and* peace*able* spirit *of Christianity.*

The hours *of* this day *are* rapid*ly* flying, *and* this occa*sion will* soon *be* passed. Neither *we* nor *our* children *can* *expect to* behold its return. *They are in the* distant regions *of* futu*rity, they* exist only *in the* all-creating *power of God*; *who shall* stand here, *a* hundred years hence, *to* trace, *through us, their* descent *from the* pilgrims, *and to* survey, *as we have* now surveyed, *the* progress *of their* country *during the* lapse *of a* century. *We* would anticipate *their* *concurrence with us in our* sentiments *of* deep regard *for* *our* common ancestors. *We* would anticipate *and* partake *the* pleasure *with which they will* then recount *the* steps of *New-England's* advance*ment. On the* morn*ing of that* day, *although it will not* disturb *us in our* repose, *the* voice *of* ac*lamation and* gratitude, *commencing on the* rock *of* Plym*outh, shall be transmitted* through millions *of the* sons *of* *the* pilgrims, till *it* lose its*elf in the* murmurs *of the* Pa*cific* seas.

We would leave, *for the consideration of* those *who shall* *then* occupy *our* places, some proof *that we* hold *the* bless-

ings transmitted from our fathers *in* just *estimation ;* some proof *of our* attachment *to the* cause *of* good govern*ment, and of* civil *and* religi*ous* liberty ; some proof *of a* sincere *and* ardent desire *to promote* every thi*ng which may* enlarge *the* understandi*ngs and* improve *the* hearts *of* men. *And when from the* long dist*ance of a* hundred years, *they shall* look back *upon us, they shall know, at* least, *that we* pos-sessed *affections, which,* runni*ng* backward, *and* warm*ing with* gratitude *for what our* ancestors *have done for our* happiness, run for*ward* also *to our* posterity, *and* meet *them* with cordial saluta*tion,* ere *yet they have* arrived *on the* shore *of* Being.

Advance, then, *ye* future gener*ations ! We* would hail *you, as you* rise *in your* long succes*sion, to* fill *the* places *which we* now fill, *and to* taste *the* blessi*ngs of* exist*ence* where *we are* passi*ng, and* soon *shall have* passed, *our* hu-man dur*ation. We* bid *you* welcome *to* this pleasant land *of the* Fathers. *We* bid *you* welcome *to the* healt*hful* skies, *and the* verdant fields *of* New-England. *We* greet *your* acces*sion to the* great inherit*ance which we have* enjoyed. *We* welcome *you to the* blessi*ngs of* good govern*ment, and* religi*ous* liberty. *We* welcome *you to the* treasures *of* sci-*ence and the* delights *of* learni*ng. We* welcome *you to the* transcend*ent* sweets *of* domestic life, *to the* happiness *of* kindred, *and* parents, *and* children. *We* welcome *you to the* immeasurable blessi*ngs of* rational exist*ence, the* im-mortal hope *of Christianity, and the* light *of everlasting* ·Truth !

EXERCISE VI.

Hospitality.—An Eastern Apologue.

Those words printed in SMALL CAPITALS, are generally omitted by Stenographers, in reporting a Speech, Lecture, Sermon, &c.

It is related in the Medrash, when king Solomon, peace be upon him, IN his early days became wicked IN THE sight OF heaven, THE Lord permitted Ashmidai THE prince OF evil spirits, TO hurl him from his throne, and to bear him many hundred leagues into A foreign country. Then THE great and glorious king Solomon became A poor and lonely wanderer over barren AND desert lands. At last he reached, fatigued and hungry, THE habitations OF man. He washed his feet, and knelt down TO thank THE God of his father David, for having preserved him through THE wilderness, and for having brought him thus far. After having humbled himself to THE Most High, he entered THE house of A rich man, TO ask for some sustenance. But he had hardly crossed THE threshhold OF THE rich man's door, when THE master OF THE house recognised him TO be king Solomon. He received him respectfully, and immediately had killed THE fattened ox, which he gave orders TO prepare for him, together with some other delicacies OF THE table. Solomon no sooner sat down TO refresh himself, than THE landlord began thus: " my dear Solomon, how camest thou to this wretched condition—in what manner hast thou lost thy great kingdom? I remember well THE time, when many thousand oxen were daily killed for THE use OF thy palace and household; there was then not A king IN the world TO be compared to thee, none as great— surely thou must have done some wicked deeds IN THE sight OF God." Then Solomon began TO weep bitterly; and could not swallow A morsel.

He rose and journeyed TO another place, where he might be unknown, and be spared untimely reproach. The following night he reached THE hut OF A poor man; "here," said Solomon, "I shall AT least be unmolested by bitter reflections and untimely admonitions." He entered THE cottage; every thing had THE appearance of poverty and misery; he had hardly seated himself when THE owner OF the hut entered from THE adjoining field, and saluted his ears with the ever welcome words of "peace be to thee," whilst at THE same time he stretched out his hand and shook that OF Solomon. He called his wife and asked her if there were any herbs prepared for THE evening repast, the good wife said that there were.

The master of THE house, although he knew Solomon, took no notice OF it, but put THE boiled herbs before THE monarch; and after he had refreshed himself, thus addressed him: "my dear king Solomon I am sorry that I can not give thee better fare, but be consoled, for him that God loveth, he chasteneth; grieve not, thou wilt ere long return to thy greatness, thy punishment is for thy own good. It is THE Holy One, blessed be his name, who hath done it. Tarry therefore with me as long as thou pleasest, eat and drink of all that THE Lord hath bestowed on me. I give it thee from all my heart; but be comforted, 'thou wilt soon be called home." Then king Solomon, peace be upon him, was rejoiced, for THE words OF THE landlord were as healing balsam to his wounded heart. And although his fare was scanty, and of the worst kind, it was sweeter to him than THE fattened ox and the delicacies OF THE rich man, who had embittered his feelings by untimely reflections. When after due afflictions and repentance, THE Lord restored Solomon to his kingdom and former greatness, he composed THE following verse, "Better is A dinner OF herbs, where love is, than a stalled ox and hatred therewith."

A FATHERS SORROW.

I bd *thee go in* grf *and* trs fr dtr *of my* hrt,
For britst dys *are* kldd oft *and* swtst jys dprt;
Th'lt fnd ths *world so* fltring nw, als! *a* vl *of* trs,
The kp *of our* xstence fld *with* sro *and with* frs.

I give thee to thy lvrs rms, *my* btful—*my* chld!
For wl *I know* thy glles hrt hs fndly *on him* smld;
He'l tk *thee to the* altr *a* yng *and* blming brid,
But hrd *I* fl *it,* ts *to* prt *with all a* fthrs prid.

I thnk *me of the* dys *gone by when on* thy mthrs brst
I usd *to* wch thy nfnt slp *and* bls thy pls *of* rst.
And oftn *in the* evntd *I* tk *thee on my* ne,
And hply *the* hrs wnt *on* amdst thy chld-hds gle.

I thnk *me of the* lving *eye of* thy yng mdn-hd,
When jyfully *to* grt *me* hm thou'st *by the* jsmn std;
And all thy gntle wrds *are* frsh, e'n nw *upon my* er,
The msik *of* thy yth *which* usd *a* fthrs hrt *to* chr.

When thy mthrs chk grw pl, *and* hr frwl ks *was* gvn
And the blsd ngl tk hr *to* lv *with God in heaven;*
How oft *I* twnd *my* fngrs *in* thy drk rvn hr,
And trsd hr ftrs *in* thy fs *and* fnd *a* prtrt *there.*

I give thee to thy lvrs rms, *my* btful—*my* chld!
For wl *I know* thy glless hrt hs fndly *on him* smld;
He'l tk *thee to the* altr *a* yng *and* blming brid,
But hrd *I* fl *it* ts *to* prt *with all a* fthrs prid.

I hp *that he will be to thee the* gd—*the* fnd—*the* trw,—
And nvr thn, thy mrig hr, *like* sm, th'lt vnly rw;
When srw's *in* thy dwling, lv, *he'l* tk *thee to* hs hrt,
And ks awy *each* btr tr *that from* thy eyelds strt.

He'l bls *the* at hs ging *out, and* at hs com-ing *in,*
And thou wlt kch *each* lk *of* lv *and* strv e'n mr *to* wn
He will be thy strnth *in* wkns, thy jy *in* srws hr,
Thy frnd bfr *a* fthless *world*—thy rn-bw *in the* shwr.

When frnds *have* fls *or* fkl prvd, *and* kr sts *on* hs brw,
When frtns lsh *is* knly flt, rmmbr thn thy vw;
And tk *him in* hs sdnd md, thy fry hnds krs,
And let him know the trsr *which in* thee *he does* pss.

Th'lt ths *be* rnd *him all* thy dys *a* tndr grsful flwr,
And he will be thy sf-grd *from the* rthless temp-st *power;*
Kls klsp thy lv *together*—be hs bty *and* hs prid,
And "the shdo of a rk" *be* thn *throughout the* dsrt wd;

I bls *thee,* then, *my* gntl grl; rsv *my* bnisn
And may the ty nw nrly wv, *be* frmd agn *in heaven;*
And thw *in* bding thee frwl, *there's* sdns *on my* brw,
I'l ld *thee to the* altr,—*God's* blsing *on* thy vw.

Ginevra.—ITALY.—ROGERS.

IF ever you should come to Modena,
(Where among other relics you may see
Tassoni's bucket—but 'tis not the true one)
Stop at a palace near the Reggio-gate,
Dwelt in of old by one of the Donati.
Its noble gardens, terrace above terrace,
And rich in fountains, statues, cypresses,
Will long detain you—but, before you go,
Enter the house—forget it not, I pray you—
And look awhile upon a picture there.

'Tis of a lady in her earliest youth,
The last of that illustrious family;
Done by Zampieri—but by whom I care not.
He, who observes it—ere he passes on,
Gazes his fill, and comes and comes again,
That he may call it up when far away.

She sits, inclining forward as to speak,
Her lips half open, and her finger up,
As though she said, "Beware!" her vest of gold
Broidered with flowers and clasped from head to foot,
An emerald stone in every golden clasp;
And on her brow, fairer than alabaster,
A coronet of pearls.

But then her face,
So lovely, yet so arch, so full of mirth,
The overflowings of an innocent heart—
It haunts me still, though many a year has fled,
Like some wild melody!

Alone it hangs
Over a mouldering heir-loom, its companion,
An oaken chest, half eaten by the worm,
But richly carved by Antony of Trent

With scripture-stories from the life of Christ;
A chest that came from Venice, and had held
The ducal robes of some old ancestor—
That by the way—it may be true or false—
But don't forget the picture ; and you will not,
When you have heard the tale they told me there.

She was an only child—her name Ginevra,
The joy, the pride of an indulgent father;
And in her fifteenth year became a bride,
Marrying an only son, Francesco Doria,
Her playmate from her birth, and her first love.

Just as she looks there in her bridal dress,
She was all gentleness, all gayety,
Her pranks the favourite theme of every tongue.
But now the day was come, the day, the hour ;
Now, frowning, smiling for the hundredth time,
The nurse, that ancient lady, preached decorum ;
And, in the lustre of her youth, she gave
Her hand, with her heart in it, to Francesco.

Great was the joy ; but at the nuptial feast,
When all sate down, the bride herself was wanting,
Nor was she to be found ! Her father cried,
" 'Tis but to make a trial of our love !"
And filled his glass to all ; but his hand shook,
And soon from guest to guest the panic spread.
'Twas but that instant she had left Francesco,
Laughing and looking back and flying still,
Her ivory tooth imprinted on his finger.
But now, alas, she was not to be found ;
Nor from that hour could any thing be guessed,
But that she was not !

Weary of his life,
Francesco flew to Venice, and embarking,

Flung it away in battle with the Turk.
Donati lived—and long might you have seen
An old man wandering as in quest of something,
Something he could not find—he knew not what.
When he was gone, the house remained awhile
Silent and tenantless—then went to strangers.

   Full fifty years were past, and all forgotten,
When on an idle day, a day of search
Mid the old lumber in the gallery,
That mouldering chest was noticed; and 'twas said
By one as young, as thoughtless as Ginevra,
" Why not remove it from its lurking-place ?"
'Twas done as soon as said; but on the way
It burst, it fell; and lo! a skeleton
With here and there a pearl, an emerald-stone,
A golden clasp, clasping a shred of gold.
All else had perished—save a wedding ring,
And a small seal, her mother's legacy,
Engraven with a name, the name of both—
" Ginevra."

      —There then had she found a grave !
Within that chest had she concealed herself.
Fluttering with joy, the happiest of the happy ;
When a spring-lock, that lay in ambush there,
Fastened her down for ever !

NUMERALS.

   Those who may prefer short-hand marks for numbers instead of figures, may adopt the following :

—	\	∕			∩	∪	(	)	∕	°	⌐o
1	2	3	4	5	6	7	8	9	0	10

Ex. ∨   23, ⌐ 50, ⌣ 601, /∩ 45032, &c. But must be distinguished from words by a dash made over the characters, thus : ⊽ 253, ⌐o 5601.

Lightning Source UK Ltd.
Milton Keynes UK
UKHW020658200521
384056UK00006B/311